WALT
DISNEY

Dreams really do

come true

JASON LILLER

Walt Disney: Dreams Really Do Come True!

Published by
Tremendous Leadership
P.O. Box 267
Boiling Springs, PA 17007

717-701-8159   1-800-233-BOOK

www.TremendousLeadership.com

ISBN: 978-1-936354-37-5

Contents

"Somehow I can't believe that there are any heights that can't be scaled by a man who knows the secrets of making dreams come true. This special secret, it seems to me, can be summarized in four C's.

They are **curiosity, confidence, courage, and constancy**."

Walt Disney

The Four C's

Imagine a world without Walt Disney— no Disney versions of classic fairy tales like *Cinderella* and *Snow White and the Seven Dwarfs*; no Disney theme parks; no Disney-inspired dreams of dancing princesses, swash-buckling pirates, and fantasy castles.

It's difficult to visualize such a place. Not only does Walt Disney touch us nearly every day, in our own homes, but the legacy of his work continues to expand and influence our lives in fields like robotics and urban plan-ning, and in the establishment of animation as a serious art form. Today, the Walt Disney Company exerts a global influence and, nearly fifty years after his death, keeps the image and words of its founder at the fore-front of its marketing and identity. There is arguably no business leader of his generation who is better recognized in the 21st century than Walt Disney.

* * *

In 1926, Walt Disney was down and out; abandoned by his employees, his livelihood taken from him, his finances on the brink of collapse. From the humblest beginnings he ascended to the pinnacle of success. How did he accomplish this remarkable achievement? And what can we learn from his experience and example?

Fortunately, Walt left us with a series of shining examples, almost providing a blue-print of strong character and good habits for those who would follow in his footsteps. He said, "Somehow I can't believe that there are any heights that can't be scaled by a man who knows the secrets of making dreams come true. This special secret, it seems to me, can be summarized in four C's. They are **curiosity**, **confidence**, **courage**, and **constancy**."

We'll look at a few episodes from his life and see how his approach to the challenges that he faced can apply to each of us.

Let's turn the calendar back to 1926 and join Walt at his Hyperion Avenue studio in Los Angeles as he faces one of the gravest challenges of his young career...

Courage

"Courage is the main quality of leadership, in my opinion, no matter where it is exercised. Usually it implies some risk—especially in new undertakings. Courage to initiate something and to keep it going; pioneering and adventurous spirit to blaze new ways, often, in our land of opportunity."

In the Hollywood of 1926, movies were silent and animated cartoons were often crude, repetitive affairs. The 25-year-old Walt Disney had by this time produced a few sponsored animated films and a successful series

"Animation can explain whatever the mind of man can conceive. This facility makes it the most versatile and explicit means of communication yet devised..."

Walt Disney

of hybrid live-action-and-animation pictures based very loosely upon *Alice in Wonderland*. Walt's distributor, Charles Mintz, had received a request from Universal Pictures for a new cartoon series, something a little different, to compete with the animated programs of rival studios. Together with his friend and collaborator, Ub Iwerks, Disney created a new character: Oswald the Lucky Rabbit.

After a little tweaking, the new character became a big hit and Disney's studio was turning out Oswald cartoons rapid-fire. Then, as now, hand-drawn animation was a labor-intensive process requiring many hours of painstaking work by skilled artists. Skilled artists cost money and Walt decided that the time had come to negotiate a little more money for his product.

With a successful film series in hand and a paying customer hungry for more, Walt journeyed to New York where he expected little trouble negotiating more favorable terms from his distributor. So imagine his reaction when Charles Mintz offered him substantially

"I have been up against tough competition all my life. I wouldn't know how to get along without it."

Walt Disney

less than he was currently paying. Walt was dumbfounded! He turned him down like any good businessman would. Then Mintz let the other shoe drop: The Oswald character was owned by Universal, not Disney, and most of Disney's animators had already been quietly hired away. A review of the contract proved, to Disney's horror, that Mintz was absolutely correct about the ownership of Oswald (you can bet that, as of that day, he paid a bit more attention to the fine print!). Oswald the Lucky Rabbit would continue as a profitable series without its creator's involvement.

The blow to Disney must have been devastating. With his business all but pulled out from under him, he could have sulked back to his studio to dwell bitterly on his defeat, at the way that his investment of time, money, and talent was taken from him in the blink of an eye. Worse, he could have thrown in the towel completely and gone back home to Missouri broken and defeated. Instead, he boarded the train to Hollywood, took his seat, and got right to work creating a new character to take Oswald's place: "I was

"*I function better when things are going badly than when they're as smooth as whipped cream.*"

Walt Disney

all alone and had nothing. Mrs. Disney and I were coming back on the train and I had to have something. I can't tell them I've lost Oswald. So I had this mouse in the back of my head…" After some input from his wife, Lillian, and a design revamp by Ub Iwerks, the remaining core of the Disney team had the vehicle that they hoped would ensure their survival: Mickey Mouse.

Had Disney allowed himself to be swayed by negativity or self-pity, it's doubtful that anyone in the 21st century would know his name. His refusal to accept these easy and all-too-human reactions, to make the effort to rise above the knee-jerk reflex that many of us would have, was the key to decisively changing his company's fortunes and it laid the foundation for the deep and diverse con-tribution that it would go on to make to American culture.

Walt said, "All the adversity I've had in my life, all my troubles and obstacles have strengthened me." It was through such set-backs that he developed the courage to

"To some people, I am kind of a Merlin who takes lots of crazy chances, but rarely makes mistakes. I've made some bad ones, but fortunately, the successes have come along fast enough to cover up the mistakes. When you go to bat as many times as I do, you're bound to get a good average."

Walt Disney

soldier on. Hopefully, very few of us will find ourselves bullied and betrayed the way that Walt was by Charles Mintz. On the other hand, maybe we could all use a little of such misfortune. After all, look where it got Walt Disney!

Confidence

"Certainly we have all had great confidence at one time in our lives, though most of us lose it as we grow older. Because of my work, I've been lucky enough to retain a shred of this useful quality..."

The popularity of Mickey Mouse and his companions, especially Donald Duck, gave Walt Disney the financial freedom to pursue other, grander ideas. Instead of sticking with animated short subjects which would have been the easy, safe thing to do, Walt chose

"In this volatile business of ours, we can ill afford to rest on our laurels, even to pause in retrospect. Times and conditions change so rapidly that we must keep our aim constantly focused on the future."

Walt Disney

to take animation where it had never gone before: the full-length feature picture.

Despite their latter-day classification as children's fare, early animated shorts were made with adult audiences in mind. Disney had already pushed the boundaries of subject matter with his series of *Silly Symphony* cartoons which were often more serious and abstract than the typical Mickey Mouse film and found that the public was receptive to the more sophisticated fare He had also successfully introduced synchronized sound (in 1928 with *Steamboat Willie*) and color (in 1932 with *Flowers and Trees*) to animation. Ready for a new challenge, he launched what was, by far, his company's most ambitious project to date: *Snow White and the Seven Dwarfs*.

Walt was betting that a well-crafted, feature-length animated film would hold the interest of a broad audience and that he could pioneer a new form of motion picture. "If we were going to get anywhere," he said, "we had to get beyond the short subject. I knew that if I could crack the feature field, I could

"*Cartoon features give us our biggest financial problems. They take a lot of manpower that could produce much more in other fields. Like most luxuries, however, there is solid value in the feature cartoon.*"

Walt Disney

really do things. *Snow White* was the answer to that." Moreover, Walt had the vision to see that animation could be more than just cheap preshow entertainment for movie patrons: it could be *art*. Today, in the age of *Toy Story* and *Beauty and the Beast*, this is a given. In the 1930s, it was revolutionary.

Walt's brother Roy, who ran the financial side of the studio, was aghast. *Snow White* would be many times more costly than the company's short-subject stock-in-trade. And it was ludicrous to assume that people would sit through a ninety-minute cartoon.

When the industry caught wind of his plans they famously dubbed the project "Disney's Folly". Even his family was against him, his own wife begging him to abandon it. Much of the advice of Roy and Lillian was motivated by fear: they felt that *Snow White* posed an existential threat to the studio and, therefore, their livelihoods. If *Snow White* failed, the company may never recover.

Needless to say, the film was a smashing success, a Hollywood blockbuster on the level

"We are not trying to entertain the critics. I'll take my chances with the public."

Walt Disney

of *Star Wars* or *Titanic*. If Walt Disney had faltered in his resolve, if he had been swayed by the doubts of the fearful, history would have been very different. Once again, everything hinged on a single decision. Without *Snow White and the Seven Dwarfs*, the legacy of the Walt Disney Company may have been nothing more than a collection of short cartoons from the '30s and '40s, historical relics frozen in time with no ongoing relevance. Walt's courage, and his insistence upon forging ahead in spite of all doubt, changed everything.

***

Trudging onward in spite of the fears and doubts of others would be a common theme throughout Disney's life. As early as the 1930's, Walt began to conceive of an amusement park based upon the studio's successful cartoon characters. Amusement parks of the period were generally crass and dirty. Walt's would be different: "When I started on Disneyland, my wife used to say, 'But why do you want to build an amusement park?

"Disneyland is a work of love. We didn't go into Disneyland just with the idea of making money."

Walt Disney

They're so dirty.' I told her that was just the point—mine wouldn't be." He also wanted to create a space where all members of the family could participate and have fun together: "I'd take [my daughters] to the merry-go-round and I took them different places and as I'd sit while they rode the merry-go-round and did all these things—sit on the bench, you know, eating peanuts—I felt that there should be something built where the parents and the children could have fun together."

Walt started to get serious about Disneyland in the early '50s. Predictably, Roy and many others at the studio were not enthused by the boss's new idea. They were running a successful motion picture business. Why on earth should they do something as risky and tawdry as an amusement park? And the expense! Disneyland cost $17,000,000 to build. *Lady and the Tramp*, which opened the same year as Disneyland, in 1955, cost an estimated $4,000,000. They could make four movies for the price of Disneyland! Besides, when it came to amusement parks, the

"I could never convince the financiers that Disneyland was feasible, because dreams offer too little collateral."

Walt Disney

Disney people had no expertise whatsoever. They had no idea how to do this successfully.

Again, Disney would not be swayed. It costs too much? Walt poured his personal fortune into it. No expertise? He hired the best engineers, artists, and architects in the country. He even turned his animators loose allowing them to contribute to the park's design. And tawdry? Once again, Walt Disney had the vision to see how the mundane could be made extraordinary. "Almost everyone warned us that Disneyland would be a Hollywood spectacular—a spectacular failure. But they were thinking about an amusement park, and we believed in our idea…" As he did with animation, proving the validity of the animated feature, so he did with the amusement park, making the quantum leap to the modern *theme park* that we take for granted today—and creating an entire industry in the process.

It's not easy to buck the advice of your family, friends, and trusted coworkers. They usually mean well. They're looking out for

"I can never stand still. I must explore and experiment. I am never satisfied with my work. I resent the limitations of my own imagination."

Walt Disney

you and your interests. But when your vision is sure and you have a clear plan of action, sometimes it's best to forge ahead in spite of all words to the contrary. Walt Disney had the confidence to do so.

Curiosity

"We don't look backwards for very long. We keep moving forward, opening new doors, and doing new things, because we are curious… and curiosity keeps leading us down new paths."

Walt Disney wasn't simply a master storyteller and filmmaker; he was an innovator who developed technologies that broke new ground, sometimes having applications that reached far beyond show business. His 1940 film *Fantasia* was a collection of animated interpretations of classical music. It

"By nature I'm an experimenter."

Walt Disney

was artistic and ambitious and no one had ever attempted anything like it before.

Fantasia promised a great visual experience, but that wasn't enough for Walt. The music was central to the presentation and he insisted that the quality of the audio surpass anything that the industry had yet seen. He wanted to put the audience right in the center of a concert hall and give them the impression that they were surrounded by the orchestra. "We know", he said, "that music emerging from one speaker behind the screen sounds thin, tinkly, and strainy. We wanted to reproduce such beautiful masterpieces as Schubert's *Ave Maria* and Beethoven's Sixth Symphony so that audiences would feel as though they were standing on the podium with [the conductor]."

What he wanted was stereophonic sound, but aside from some experimentation, no one had yet developed such a thing. Once Walt's curiosity was fired, there was no stopping him. He hired engineers to study the problem and took a personal interest in the solution.

"I believe in being an innovator."

Walt Disney

A number of innovations were required to accomplish such an ambitious project. Microphones were set up at strategic locations around the orchestra to capture and record the sounds that emerged from each section. The sound-mixing process required the creation of new technologies that simply didn't exist. For example, how would they control cross-fades, the traveling of sound from one speaker to the next? Today this would be handled electronically, but that was not an option in the late 1930s. Walt and his engineers solved this problem by improvising a mechanical system out of *bicycle chains and dimmer switches*.

Disney dubbed his sound system *Fantasound* and he won a special Academy Award for its development, even though it would be years before stereo sound would really take hold in the nation's movie houses.

***

Almost a decade later, in 1949, Walt purchased a lifelike mechanical bird. Immediately grasping its potential, he gave the toy

"I'm just very curious—got to find out what makes things tick..."

Walt Disney

to one of his engineers, Roger Broggie, and told him to pick it apart. His mission: figure out how it worked and how they could improve and expand its technology to do bigger and better things.

After analyzing the mechanism, Roger and Walt used their newfound knowledge to build a miniature robotic dancing man from scratch, with Disney himself building many of the parts. They used *that* experience to develop a Disneyland attraction called *The Enchanted Tiki Room* which featured over 150 robotic birds and plants—the first of Disney's famous audio-animatronic figures.

But this was just a waypoint on the journey to their real goal: the creation of a fully lifelike human figure. In 1962 Robert Moses, president of the 1964/1965 New York World's Fair, toured the Disney workshop and saw a rudimentary animatronic figure of Abraham Lincoln for an attraction that would eventually become Walt Disney World's *The Hall of Presidents*. Moses decided that the Lincoln figure was just the thing

"Everyone needs deadlines. Even the beavers. They loaf around all summer, but when they are faced with the winter deadline, they work like fury. If we didn't have deadlines, we'd stagnate."

Walt Disney

to have at the fair and Walt agreed—even though his engineers said that there was no way the project could be ready by 1964. "I figured it would take me ten years to get Mr. Lincoln going", he said. In fact, he had about thirteen months. Disney tackled the problem by engaging his staff in a way that he had done many times in the past: I know you can do it. Figure it out.

They did figure it out: Great Moments With Mr. Lincoln opened on time and was one of the most talked-about exhibits at the fair. It went on to have a long life at Disneyland where you can still enjoy it today nearly fifty years after its debut.

These stories of scrappy industriousness are examples of remarkable ingenuity, but the driving force behind ingenuity is curiosity: putting a robust, inquisitive mind to work to fully understand the problems (how do we create a synchronized multichannel movie soundtrack? How do we create a fully-lifelike mechanical human being?) and devise practical solutions.

"There's really no secret about our approach. We keep moving forward—opening up new doors and doing new things—because we're curious. And curiosity keeps leading us down new paths. We're always exploring and experimenting."

Walt Disney

Walt Disney was intensely curious and understood how to harness his curiosity to achieve great things: "We keep moving forward—opening up new doors and doing new things—because we're curious. And curiosity keeps leading us down new paths. We're always exploring and experimenting." When you feel that questioning itch—how does that work? What does that do?—take the time to follow that path and ask yourself how you can use the information that you discover.

Constancy

"We share, to a large extent, one another's fate. We help create those circumstances which favor or challenge us in meeting our objectives and realizing our dreams. There is great comfort and inspiration in this feeling of close human relationships and its bearing on our mutual fortunes—a powerful force to overcome the 'tough breaks' which are certain to come to most of us from time to time."

Walt Disney's fourth C is constancy. Constancy   can   have   two   distinct

"I'd like to add one thought to the subject of success and the claims made for it as a deserved reward for effort and understanding. It seems to me shallow and arrogant for any man in these times to claim he is completely self-made, that he owes all his success to his own unaided efforts. While, of course, it is basic Americanism that a man's standing is in part due to his personal enterprise and capacity, it is equally true that many hands and hearts and minds generally contribute to anyone's notable achievement."

Walt Disney

meanings—Walt didn't elaborate, but either one would fit his character.

Constancy is fidelity: being faithful to the people with whom you work. Disney was renowned for the family-like atmosphere that he instilled at his studio which provided some of the best working conditions in motion pictures. Disney employees were rarely dismissed and rarely left. There was a place for anyone who was willing to work hard and for anyone who had something to contribute. If things weren't working out for you in your current position, the company would give you the opportunity to try other jobs until you found one at which you excelled.

Many Disney staff were employed for decades. "No matter what the provocation", Walt said, "I never fire a man who is honestly trying to deliver a job. Few workers who become established at the Disney studio ever leave voluntarily or otherwise, and many have been on the payroll all their working lives."

"If I were a fatalist, or a mystic, which I decidedly am not, it might be appropriate to say I believe in my lucky star. But I reject 'luck'——I feel every person creates his own 'determinism' by discovering his best aptitudes and following them undeviatingly."

Walt Disney

Even though Walt was sometimes betrayed by the very employees about whom he so deeply cared (most notably when Charles Mintz hired away his staff in 1926, as discussed earlier, and during a major animator's strike in 1941) he refused to become bitter and cynical. He steadfastly maintained his loyalty to his people.

***

Constancy is steadiness. Walt Disney's work ethic was unparalleled. No challenge was too great to stop him and no success was big enough to lull him into complacency. Many people experience their greatest triumphs early in their lives. For Disney, his greatest triumphs arguably came late in his career with the opening of Disneyland and the groundbreaking film *Mary Poppins*. This wasn't the result of luck or circumstance; it was the product of hard work and intelligent planning, of doggedly plowing through all problems, challenges, and discouragements.

In fact, this second definition of constancy is the common thread that runs

"*All our dreams can come true if we have the courage to pursue them.*"

Walt Disney

throughout Walt Disney's life and through-out the history of the Walt Disney Company during its founder's lifetime: an unwavering dedication to outdoing himself, to providing a product of exceptional value, to creating sights, sounds, and experiences that no one had ever before known. Even on his deathbed in 1966, weary and in pain, he was actively planning his greatest project: EPCOT. His vision was not of the theme park that eventually took root at Walt Disney World in 1982, but of a real, living city—an **E**xperimental **P**rototype **C**ommunity of **T**omorrow—that would have pioneered new concepts in virtually every area of human life: urban planning, transportation, business, industry, recreation, and sustainable living.

EPCOT was ahead of its time in 1966. Maybe it's ahead of its time now. But Walt saw it. Had he lived a few more years, we would have seen it, too. It would be a thriving city filled with marvels that, sadly, we will never know. Walt Disney had the curiosity, confidence, courage, and constancy to make his dreams come true.

"There are fashions in reading, even in thinking. You don't have to follow them unless you want to. On the other hand, watch out! Don't stick too closely to your favorite subject. That would keep you from adventuring into other fields. It's silly to build a wall around your interests."

Walt Disney

Bibliography

Capodagli, Bill, and Lynn Jackson. *The Disney Way Fieldbook: How to Implement Walt Disney's Vision of Dream, Believe, Dare, Do in Your Own Company.* New York: McGraw-Hill, 2001.

Greene, Katherine and Richard Greene. *Inside the Dream: The Personal Story of Walt Disney.* New York: Disney Editions, 2001.

The Imagineers. *Walt Disney Imagineering: A Behind the Dreams Look at Making the Magic Real.* New York: Hyperion, 1996.

The Quotable Walt Disney. New York: Disney Editions, 2001.

Thomas, Bob. *Walt Disney: An American Original.* New York: Disney Editions, 1976.

Williams, Pat, with Jim Denney. *How to Be Like Walt: Capturing the Disney Magic Every Day of Your Life.* Deerfield Beach: Health Communications, Inc., 2004.

Read more excellent titles from our Life-Changing Classics Series
available at www.TremendousLeadership.com

3 Therapies of Life (The), by Charlie "Tremendous" Jones; Foreword by Dr. Tracey C. Jones.

7 Golden Rules of Milton Hershey (The), by Greg Rothman; Foreword by Richard Zimmerman.

7 Leadership Virtues of Joan of Arc (The), by Peter Darcy.

Acres of Diamonds, by Russell H. Conwell; Appreciation by John Wanamaker.

Advantages of Poverty, by Andrew Carnegie; Foreword by Dale Carnegie.

As a Man Thinketh, by James Allen.

Books Are Tremendous, edited by Charlie "Tremendous" Jones; Introduction by J.C. Penney.

"Bradford, You're Fired!", by William W. Woodbridge.

Breakthrough Speaking, by Mark Sanborn.

Character Building, by Booker T. Washington.

Discipleship, by John M. Segal

From Belfast to Narnia: The Life and Faith of C.S. Lewis, by The C.S. Lewis Institute.

Greatest Thing in the World (The), by Henry Drummond; Introduction by Dwight L. Moody.

Key to Excellence (The), by Charlie "Tremendous" Jones.

Kingship of Self-Control (The), by William George Jordan; Foreword by Charlie "T" Jones.

Lincoln Ideals (The), edited by Charlie "Tremendous" Jones.

Luther on Leadership, by Stephen J. Nichols.

Maxims of Life & Business, by John Wanamaker; Forewords by Elbert Hubbard and Russell Conwell.

Message to Garcia (A), by Elbert Hubbard.

My Conversion, by Charles Spurgeon; Edited & Compiled by Charlie "T" Jones.

Mystery of Self-Motivation (The), by Charlie "Tremendous" Jones.

New Common Denominator of Success (The), by Albert E.N. Gray; Foreword by Charlie "Tremendous" Jones.

Price of Leadership (The), by Charlie "Tremendous" Jones; foreword by Dr. Tracey C. Jones.

Reason Why (The), by R.A. Laidlaw; Introduction by Marjorie Blanchard.

Ronald Wilson Reagan: The Great Communicator, by Greg Rothman.

Self-Improvement through Public Speaking, by Orison Swett Marden; Introduction by Forrest Wallace Cato.

Science of Getting Rich: Abridged Edition (The), by Wallace D. Wattles; edited by Charlie "T" Jones.

Succeeding With What You Have, by Charles Schwab; Foreword by Andrew Carnegie.

That Something, by William W. Woodbridge; Introduction by Paul J. Meyer.

Three Decisions (The), by Charlie "Tremendous" Jones; Foreword by Dr. Tracey C. Jones.

Walt Disney: Dreams Really Do Come True!, by Jason Liller.

Wit and Wisdom of General George S. Patton (The), compiled by Charlie "T." Jones.